**Helping Children See Jesus**

ISBN: 978-1-64104-069-3

*God the Trinity, Worthy of*
# Worship
*New Testament Volume 43:
Revelation Part 2*

Author: Ruth B. Greiner
Illustrator: Vernon Henkel and Frances H. Hertzler
Computer Graphic Artist: Ed Olson
Typesetting and Layout: Patricia Pope

© 2018 Bible Visuals International
PO Box 153, Akron, PA 17501-0153
Phone: (717) 859-1131
www.biblevisuals.org

All rights reserved. No part of this publication may be reproduced, stored in a retrieval system or transmitted in any form by any means, electronic, mechanical, photocopy, recording or otherwise, without the prior permission of the publisher, except as provided by USA copyright law.

## RELATED ITEMS

To access related items (such as activities, memory verse posters and translated texts) please visit our web store at shop.biblevisuals.org and enter 1043 in the search box on the page.

## FREE TEXT DOWNLOAD

To access a FREE printable copy of the teaching text (PDF format) in English or other available languages, enter S1043DL in the search box. Add the item to your cart, and use coupon code XTACSV17 at checkout. Once your order is processed you will receive an email with a link to the free download.

Thou art worthy, O Lord, to receive glory and honor and power; for Thou hast created all things, and for Thy pleasure they are and were created. Revelation 4:11

# Lesson 1
# THE THRONE IN HEAVEN

## NOTE TO THE TEACHER

Revelation is sometimes called the "Throne Book," for the word *throne* is mentioned about 40 times. In this first lesson, we are introduced to the throne of God. His throne is eternal. God is on His throne and He is ruling over all. Take time to read the third chapter of Habakkuk and see a similar picture of the God of Light. Note especially Habakkuk 3:3-4.

The Apostle John was nearing the end of his life on earth. Can you imagine the thrill he had when God caught him up to see Heaven? John probably understood the symbols which God used to show him the future. Usually they will be clear to us if we check other Scriptures where the same symbols are used. For example, in this lesson we learn of 24 elders. In the New Testament, elders–the highest officials in the church–represent the whole church. (See Acts 15:6; 20:28.) It is likely, therefore, that these 24 elders represent all the redeemed. The elders are crowned with golden crowns. Here the Greek word translated as *crown* is the same as the word is used to refer to the believers' rewards.

(See 1 Corinthians 9:25; 1 Thessalonians 2:19; 2 Timothy 4:8; James 1:12; 1 Peter 5:4.) They have white clothes as attributed to the saints in Revelation 3:5, 18. So we believe the elders represent all redeemed human beings–not angels.

If you have a *Pilgrim or Scofield* edition of the Bible, be sure to study all the footnotes for the book of Revelation. We urge you to get a copy of the New Testament section of the *Ryrie Study Bible*. This is available in paperback, with either the King James or New American Standard version. The notes throughout, and especially those on Revelation, will help make the verses clear.

Remember. . . beginning with this section and continuing through the end of the book, the events are all in the future. ("The things which shall be hereafter"–Revelation 1:19.) It was necessary for John to see the throne in Heaven before seeing the terrible judgments which will come to the earth. Go slowly enough so your students will have clear understanding of the things which will take place in the future.

**Scripture to be studied:** Revelation 4:1-5

**The *aim* of the lesson:** To teach that long ago, God showed John what He wants us to know about the future.

**What your students should *know*:** God always keeps His word, promises of reward and warnings of judgment.

**What your students should *feel*:** An expectancy of the fulfillment of God's promises.

**What your students should *do*:**
 *Unsaved:* Place their trust in Christ today.
 *Saved:* Make certain they are living now to please God so when they face the Lord they will not have regrets.

**Lesson outline (for the teacher's and students' notebooks):**
1. A door to Heaven opened (Revelation 4:1).
2. God on His throne (Revelation 4:2-3).
3. Twenty-four thrones around God's throne (Revelation 4:4).
4. Seven lamps of fire burning before God's throne (Revelation 4:5).

**The verse to be memorized:**

*Thou art worthy, O Lord, to receive glory and honor and power, for Thou hast created all things, and for Thy pleasure they are and were created.* (Revelation 4:11)

## THE LESSON:

John, the beloved apostle, was a prisoner on the Island of Patmos, far away from his friends. Although he was alone, he was comforted by the presence of God. Also God showed him things which no one else saw. One of the most glorious sights was that of the Lord Jesus. John would never forget it. He had seen the shining face of the Son of God, His flaming eyes, His powerful hands, His glowing feet. And John had heard His majestic, mighty voice saying, "Write the things which you have seen, the things which are now, and the things which will be after this" (Revelation 1:19).

John was quick to obey. He wrote of having seen the Lord Christ. He wrote of things which were happening in seven of the Asian churches during his time. But what about the things still to come? How could he write about something which had not yet happened?

There is only One who knows the future. That One is God. God knows everything about the past, the present, *and* the future. So God did something marvelous. He showed John the future things which are yet to happen. Imagine seeing future happenings!

## 1. A DOOR TO HEAVEN OPENED
### Revelation 4:1

### Show Illustration #1

John looked up and saw a door opened in Heaven. Perhaps he quickly remembered something Christ Jesus had said before He died: "I will be with you only a little longer. Then I must leave you. You will look for Me. But you cannot come where I am going" (John 13:33, 36).

One of His disciples (Simon Peter) had asked, "Where are You going? I want to follow You."

Jesus answered, "You're not able to follow Me now. But you will follow Me later."

Then Jesus said, "Do not let your heart be troubled. I am going away to prepare a place for you. And if I go and prepare a place for you, I will come again and take you to Myself; that where I am there you may be also." (See John 14:1-3.)

John remembered having heard those words. The Lord had gone away as He had said He would. But He had promised to come back. When would this be? Jesus had not revealed the day or the hour of His coming. But He had commanded, "Watch and be ready" For He said He might return at any time.

How would He come back? John wondered about that, as did the other disciples. Many of the believers also had questions about Christ's coming. The Christians needed more information. That is why another apostle of Jesus Christ (Paul) wrote, "Brothers, this is what the Lord says. He Himself will come from Heaven with a mighty shout, with the voice of the archangel, and with the trumpet of God. Believers in Christ who have died will rise first.

Then we who are still alive on earth will be caught up with them in the clouds to meet the Lord in the air. And we shall be with the Lord forever." (See 1 Thessalonians 4:13-18.)

Yes, the Lord Jesus Christ will come again. We don't know when. But just as surely as He came the first time to Bethlehem, He will come again. John looked forward to this. There on the Isle of Patmos, seeing the open door, perhaps John thought Christ Jesus might return that very moment.

As he looked, John heard a voice commanding, "Come up here. I'll show you a vision of what will happen in the future."

John didn't have to ask permission to leave the island. He didn't have to call for someone to unlock his chains. Immediately, by the power of God's Spirit, he was taken right to Heaven. Think of that!

## 2. GOD ON HIS THRONE
### Revelation 4:2-3

### Show Illustration #2

Up in Heaven, John saw a beautiful throne. Seated on it is God the Father in all His bright, dazzling glory. It was impossible for John to describe the scene. All he can say is that the One who sits there shines like precious jewels. The glow made John think of a jasper stone (a reminder of God's holiness and glory). He thought too of a blood-red sardine stone (speaking of a blood sacrifice).

The throne upon which God sits is a throne of power, for God *rules* over *all*. From the throne comes lightning and thundering. (See Revelation 4:5a.) This is a reminder that God's throne is also a throne of *judgment*. Since God is holy, He must judge all sin–the sin of each man, woman, boy and girl–unless it has been forgiven and cleansed through faith in Jesus Christ. This judgment is to come upon the earth, as John would soon learn. The judgment spoken of here is not the final judgment of hell, but the judgment of the yet future Tribulation period.

Around the throne John sees a *rainbow*, a complete circle–the color of a light green emerald stone. It is much different from the rainbows we see on earth, which are usually only part of a circle.

The green rainbow around God's throne reminds us that God keeps His promises. Thousands of years ago God made a rainbow and set it in the sky. It helped Noah (and all people since then) to remember that God would never again send a flood over the whole earth to destroy it. God has kept that promise. He *always* keeps His promises. He is faithful. Because He is holy, He must punish sin. But He is also merciful; so He offers forgiveness to all who will accept the Lord Jesus Christ, His Son, as the sacrifice for sin.

Have you accepted that sacrifice? Have you received Christ Jesus into your heart and life? Is He your Saviour? If He is, you need not fear the terrible judgment to come.

## 3. TWENTY-FOUR THRONES AROUND GOD'S THRONE
### Revelation 4:4

### Show Illustration #3

Up in Heaven, John sees 24 thrones around the throne of God. Sitting on these thrones are 24 elders. They are wearing white robes and golden crowns. Think for a moment: Do you remember from our previous lessons some of the rewards God promised to each Christian believer?

1. A crown of life (Revelation 2:10)
2. Reigning with Jesus (Revelation 3:21)
3. A white robe (Revelation 3:18)

John could look closely at these elders. He could see the crowns on their heads and the white robes. These 24 represent all the believers, the redeemed overcomers who have placed their trust in the Lord Christ. They're on thrones just as the Lord promised. They are wearing crowns exactly as He had said they would. And they have white robes. God surely keeps His promises!

All the believers (represented by the 24 elders) are safe in Heaven forevermore, even though from the throne come flashes of lightning and crashes of thunder. These speak of judgments soon to come to men and women, boys and girls, who reject Jesus Christ as Saviour.

## 4. SEVEN LAMPS OF FIRE BURNING BEFORE GOD'S THRONE
### Revelation 4:5

### Show Illustration #4

In front of the throne, John sees seven lamps of fire. These burning lamps are reminders of God the Holy Spirit in His fullness and power. (He is sometimes referred to as the seven-fold Spirit of God– see Revelation 1:4; 3:1; 5:6; compare with Isaiah 11:2.)

Remember that God is a tri-unity (or trinity). He is *three* persons *in one*: God the Father, God the Son, and God the Holy Spirit.

John has already told us of seeing God the Father on His throne in Heaven. Here he speaks of God the Holy Spirit in Heaven, represented by the seven flaming lamps. In the next lessons we will learn that God the Son is also in Heaven.

You and I haven't seen Heaven. But we can know the living God of Heaven. And, wonder of wonders, He who is in Heaven can at the same time live in your heart and mine! He enters our lives when we place our trust in His Son, the Lord Jesus Christ. His Spirit lives within us and tells us when we do wrong. (See John 16:7-11.) This blessed Holy Spirit of God also comforts us like a warm, glowing fire. (See John 14:16-18.) And He guides us and gives us power to serve God. (See Acts 1:8.)

But this same Holy Spirit also convicts people of sin. He warns of the coming judgment. (See John 16: 7-11.)

Today God is on His throne in Heaven. He is in control of everything. He will always reign on His throne. But some future day–and it may be soon–all who have trusted in the Lord Christ will also reign with Him. (Show Illustration #3.) Those who have not believed in the Saviour will suffer the fiery judgment of God. Your future (after life is over) depends upon what you do now. If you receive Christ as your Saviour from sin, God will receive you into His beautiful home in Heaven. If you don't receive the Lord Jesus here on earth, God will not receive you into His heavenly home. Indeed, you will be separated from God and suffer His judgment forever and ever. If you have not placed your trust in the Lord Jesus Christ, will you do so right now?

If you are already His child, write down the name of one who is not in the family of God. Ask the Lord to give you opportunity this week to introduce this person to Christ the Saviour. Now check on your own life: are you living in such a way that you will not have regrets throughout eternity?

**ASSIGNMENT:** Between now and our next class session, read Revelation 4:1-11 as often as possible.

# Lesson 2
# PERFECT WORSHIP

## NOTE FOR THE TEACHER

Are you blessed as you study and teach the marvelous truths of the *Revelation of Jesus Christ*? This book is primarily for those who are in God's family through faith in His Son. By knowing the teaching of Revelation, we can be kept from making mistakes about the person of Christ, His power and His program. There is no book in the Bible like it! Its details are encouraging to the child of God. Seeing the Lamb of God (who had been slain) on the throne prepares us for another day's battle, assured that the Lord reigns forever!

There are a number of interesting symbols in the book. Many of these can be plainly understood. Some are explained. Some are not. This is also true in other parts of Scripture. For example, look at Psalm 22, written hundreds of years before the crucifixion of our Lord. Verse 18 contains a prophecy of casting lots for Christ's garment. (Compare John 19:23-24.) This was an exact statement. In the same Psalm, verses 12 and 13, there are symbols which are not explained. But they are perfectly clear. The bulls and lions are understood to be the fierce enemies of the Lord.

As we shall see in a later study, the sun, moon, stars, day and night will be affected by God's judgment. (See Revelation 8:12.) The stars are actually those in the heavens. Later, however, we're told that a star falls from Heaven. (See Revelation 9:1-2.) The text itself indicates that this star is a created being (probably an angel). So the word *star* has two meanings. This is not unusual. Even in English we speak of the stars in the heavens. But we may have an athlete who is the "star" of his team. This is a symbol with a perfectly plain meaning.

We don't claim to be able to explain symbols with *perfect* certainty. In these volumes we are using what we *believe* to be the explanations of the symbols. And we have tried to be consistent in the matter of plainly interpreting the symbols.

Your students will need help in remembering the meanings of the symbols. We suggest that you use several large sheets of paper. On each one print the name of one symbol. On the reverse side, print the meaning of that symbol. Urge your students to write the *meaning* of each symbol beside of the symbol in the margins of their Bibles.

In the first two lessons we have:

24 elders on thrones = *representatives of all who believe in Christ*
4 living beings = *angels*, perhaps
7 lamps burning = *the Holy Spirit*

According to Isaiah 11:2, the Holy Spirit has seven qualities of perfection. He is:

the Spirit of the Lord
the Spirit of wisdom
the Spirit of understanding
the Spirit of counsel
the Spirit of might
the Spirit of knowledge
the Spirit of the reverent fear of the Lord

Before each lesson, review the symbols which have been used previously.

The four living creatures mentioned in this lesson (Revelation 4:6) may be angels, perhaps cherubim. Many see similarities between the four living ones and the portrayals of Christ by the Gospel writers. According to Matthew, He is the Lion of the tribe of Judah: the King. Mark speaks of Him as the Servant who became the sacrifice for sin. (The calf was a sacrificial animal–see Hebrews 9:12, 19.) Luke emphasizes that He is the Son of Man. To John, He is the One who came down from the heights of Heaven, stayed with us awhile, then went back to the heights from which He came. The flying eagle links Christ with Heaven.

The book of Revelation is important. And like all of Scripture, a study of it should affect our lives. (See 2 Timothy 3:16-17.) Indeed, God promises happiness to those who read and keep the sayings of the book. (See Revelation 1:3; 22:7.) So study this book, teacher. Arrange your life according to it. Get the blessing God wants you to have.

---

**Scripture to be studied:** Revelation 4:6-11

**The *aim* of the lesson:** To show that the worship of God is as important on earth as it is in Heaven.

**What your students should *know*:** The triune God is worthy of all worship.

**What your students should *feel*:** A desire to honor and worship God.

**What your students should *do*:** Worship God willingly and at all times. Offer their lives to Him for loving service.

**Lesson outline (for the teacher's and students' notebooks):**
1. The crystal sea before God's throne (Revelation 4:6a).
2. The living ones around God's throne (Revelation 4: 6b-9).
3. The 24 elders worship God (Revelation 4: 10a).
4. The golden crowns are given to God (Revelation 4:10b-11).

**The verse to be memorized:**

*Thou art worthy, O Lord, to receive glory and honor and power, for Thou hast created all things, and for Thy pleasure they are and were created. (Revelation 4:11)*

## THE LESSON

John was up in Heaven in the very presence of His Creator, God, the One who made all things. On earth, John had worshiped God. Now he saw Him in all His power and glory on His throne in Heaven. There was so much to see in Heaven that John took it in slowly.

## Show Illustration #2

Looking at the throne, John saw a beautiful emerald rainbow. It was different from any rainbow he had seen on earth. This rainbow is a complete circle going all the way around the throne. What a beautiful picture of God, the completely faithful One, and of never-ending life!

## Show Illustration #3

Then John saw more thrones–24 of

them–around God's throne. Sitting on them were 24 elders, representing the redeemed believers (the overcomers). Each wore a white robe and a golden crown. What an honor f\or them to sit on thrones, wearing crowns in the presence of almighty God!

### Show Illustration #4

Nearby, seven lamps glowed with blazing flames. These are reminders of the Holy Spirit of God in His perfect fullness. And there was the noise of thunder. John could see flashes of lightning coming from the throne. But the believers on their thrones were not afraid.

## 1. THE CRYSTAL SEA BEFORE GOD'S THRONE
### Revelation 4:6a

### Show Illustration #5

In front of the throne of God John sees a sea which looks like glass. It is clear as crystal–pure, holy and bright. John had never seen anything like it. On earth he was on the Sea of Galilee many times. Often storms had come up, making the water rough and dangerous. But no such thing can happen in Heaven. Even the thunder and lightning do not disturb the glassy sea. The water is clear and smooth. It is not impure like the seas of earth. And this water is not needed for washing or to make people clean. In Heaven there is no need for washing. Everyone there is pure and clean.

How different this is from the earth! Men and women on earth need to be cleansed. That is why King Solomon, who lived long before John, had a large brass laver (basin) placed in his magnificent temple. The water in the basin was used by the priests. They washed their hands and feet before they entered the holy place. They had to be clean before they could worship and serve the Lord. That huge basin held enough water for 2,000 baths. The priests had to wash themselves again and again. (See 1 Kings 7:23-26.)

## 2. THE LIVING ONES AROUND GOD'S THRONE
### Revelation 4: 6b-9

John turns from looking at the wonderful sea up in Heaven and glances again at the throne.

### Show Illustration #6

There John sees four living beings. They look something like creatures he had seen on earth. Yet they are different.

The first one is like a lion. The second is like a calf. The third has a face like a man. And the fourth is like a flying eagle. Each of the four living beings have six wings. They are full of eyes.

From what John has told us about these strange-looking creatures we can only imagine how they must have looked.

Remember, these creatures are not statues. They are not made of stone or marble. They are living, moving beings. On earth, if we saw a strange creature with many eyes, we would probably be frightened. But in Heaven there is no fear. There is nothing there to hurt or harm anyone. Imagine being near a wild-looking friendly animal that won't hurt you!

What are these creatures near God's throne in Heaven? We're not certain. They may be angels. (Cherubim, perhaps. Compare to Ezekiel 10:15-20.) Why are they there? Did God want the believers in Heaven to worship these beings? Oh, no! On earth some men and women do make statues of animals or other things and worship them. By doing so, they disobey God. But in Heaven there is no disobedience. God is the only One who is worshiped. Why then are the creatures there? Because they have something important to do. Day and night they cry out: "Holy, holy, holy, is the Lord God, the Almighty, who was, and who is, and who is to come!" (Compare with Isaiah 6:3.)

They are praising Almighty God, the ruler of all. Did you notice they said, "Holy" three times? This was because they were praising the trinity–God the Three-in-One. God the Father is holy. (See Psalm 145:17; Habakkuk 1:12-13a.) God the Son is holy. (See Luke 1:35; 4:34.) No one could find any sin in Him (John 8:46). And God the Spirit is holy. (See Luke 1:35.) Even His name–the Holy Spirit–tells us so.

## 3. THE TWENTY-FOUR ELDERS WORSHIP GOD
### Revelation 4:10a

### Show Illustration #7

As John watched and listened, the 24 elders, who had been seated around the throne rose to their feet and worshipped the Three-in-One God. No one else in Heaven or earth is worthy to be worshiped and praised. These 24 (representing all believers) rose from their thrones and fell down before God's throne to worship Him.

## 4. THE GOLDEN CROWNS ARE GIVEN TO GOD
### Revelation 4:10b-11

### Show Illustration #8

Then, to show their gratitude and love for God, the redeemed ones take off their crowns and offer them before His throne. They give their treasures in loving worship. Together they exclaim, "You are worthy, O Lord, to receive glory and honor and power; for You have created all things, and for Your pleasure they are and were created."

"Worship" means to bow before One whose worth is known. God is worthy of all praise. He created all things. Each person (you and I), each animal, each bird, each insect, each mountain, each tree, each flower–each was created for His pleasure. You and I, while here on earth, can bring the greatest pleasure to God by obeying Him and worshiping Him gladly, regularly and willingly.

Is God pleased with you today? Do you praise and honor and give glory to Him for all He is? Or do you simply thank Him for things He gives? He wants you to thank Him for everything. (See 1 Thessalonians 5:18.)

Would you like to bow and worship God right now? Together let us pray the words of our memory verse: "Thou art worthy, O Lord, to receive glory and honor and power, for Thou hast created all things and for Thy pleasure they are and were created."

Speak to Him reverently, remembering His greatness and glory. Speak praise for His power, shown by His creating everything. Thank Him for His wonderful plan of salvation. In Heaven, the believers who have seen the eternal God on His throne, throw themselves down before the Lord and worship Him. When we are up there, we, too, will fall before the glory of God. And we will give Him all the honor that is due Him.

If we truly love Him, however, we will worship Him here on earth. And our lives will honor Him. Are you taking time, each day, to worship God and praise Him? If not, will you promise Him right now that from this day on you will worship Him every day? You may not have a golden crown to give Him. But you can offer your life to serve Him. Are you willing to do that right now?

**ASSIGNMENT:** Study Revelation 5:1-14 as often as possible. Write down the four main truths that appear in that section.

# Lesson 3
# THE SCROLL

## NOTE TO THE TEACHER

This is a choice chapter in the book of Revelation. On His throne in Heaven, God holds in His hand His program for the future. John is sad. He fears that no one is worthy to take the scroll. Its seals must be broken so that God's program can be carried out on the earth.

Then the Lamb of God appears. He has waited until everyone else has eliminated himself from the right to take the scroll. He alone is worthy to accept the scroll and to loosen the seals. What a thrill–the scroll in the hands of the Son of God! He will open the seals one by one and the marvelous programs of God will take place. This is enough to make all creation offer Him praise and adoration. God's purposes will be fulfilled. In spite of the strange and perplexing events which will follow, God is on the throne. He rules forever!

The emphasis of this fifth chapter of Revelation is on the scroll and the One who receives it. In this lesson your students should not be told what is written on the scroll.

But you, teacher, should know. For your own preparation, study chapters five through eleven. The day is coming when Christ the Redeemer will reign over everything forever. (See Revelation 11:15.)

It is sobering to think that there is One in Heaven who will always have the marks of death on Him. (See Revelation 5:6. Compare with Luke 24:40; John 2:20-21.) All through eternity we'll be reminded of the great cost of our redemption. Indeed, in Heaven His death will be the subject of our praise. (See Revelation 5:9, 12.) May your life, and the lives of those you reach, be filled with daily praise for Him, His death, and His resurrection.

If you live in an area where printed programs are not used, you will want to change the opening of the lesson. You may show them the program you have for this class session. The list of things you have to do during the week is your own personal program. You may prefer to show them this list.

**Scripture to be studied:** Revelation 5:1-14

**The *aim* of the lesson:** To show that God the Father gives the highest honor to the Lord Jesus Christ and so should we.

**What your students should *know*:** God has foretold that a day will come when everyone will kneel before the Lord Jesus Christ.

**What your students should *feel*:** Gratitude that Jesus Christ gave His life for all.

**What your students should *do*:** Right now give to God the glory, honor and praise that He deserves. Confess anything that is not a praise to Him.

**Lesson outline (for the teacher's and students' notebooks):**

1. The important scroll (Revelation 5:1-4).
2. The worthy Lamb (Revelation 5:5-7).
3. The new song (Revelation 5:8-10).
4. The worshipful creation (Revelation 5:11-14).

**The verse to be memorized:**

*Thou art worthy, O Lord, to receive glory and honor and power, for Thou hast created all things, and for Thy pleasure they are and were created.* (Revelation 4:11)

## THE LESSON

Have you ever attended a Christmas play or a concert where they had printed programs? If you arrived early enough, you could study the program and know exactly what was about to happen. Much of the book of Revelation, beginning with chapter four, tells us what God is going to do in the future. If you have done your assignment for this class, you know that when John visited Heaven, he saw a book. In the book are seven events in God's program (events which haven't taken place yet). But John couldn't study the program. He had to wait until One who was worthy could be found to loosen the seals. And the seven seals, we shall see, could not be taken off at one time.

## 1. THE IMPORTANT SCROLL
### Revelation 5:1-4

The book John saw in Heaven was a scroll. It was a roll of parchment full of writing on both sides.

John was eager to know what was going to happen in God's program. Then he heard a strong angel voice calling out, "Who is worthy to open the scroll and loosen the seals?" John waited eagerly for someone to step forward. But no one in Heaven or on earth or under the earth was pure enough to open the scroll–or even to look at it! No one–no angel, no man, not one of the living creatures, not even any of the elders–was worthy.

Could it be that the seals would not be broken? Will the program and purposes of God not be fulfilled?

## Show Illustration #9

John cried bitterly. He was distressed because no one could be found who was worthy to look at the scroll or open it. Then one of the elders said, "Do not weep. Look! The Lion from the tribe of Judah, the Root of David, has won the right to open the scroll and its seven seals."

Who is the "Lion from the tribe of Judah, the Root of David"? He is Jesus Christ the Lord. (Compare Genesis 49:10.) Mary, the mother of the Lord Jesus, was of the tribe of Judah. And Christ is a descendant of David. (See Psalm 110:1; Matthew 22:41-45; compare to Matthew 1:1, Isaiah 11:1, 10.) Jesse was David's father, according to 1 Samuel 17:12.)

Not only did the Lord Jesus Christ come from the family line of David, but also is David's Lord and King. (See Luke 20:41-44; Acts 2:34-36.) He, the noble Lion of the tribe of Judah, is King. He alone has the right to take the scroll and break the seals.

John looked up and was surprised, for he didn't see a lion.

## 2. THE WORTHY LAMB
### Revelation 5:5-7

Instead, he saw between the throne (with the four living creatures) and the elders, a Lamb. Could this be the same person the elder spoke of? Yes, He is the same–the Lord Jesus Christ. For Jesus, Son of God, is not only all powerful; He is also meek, as a lamb.

Looking more closely, John sees that although the Lamb is standing, He looks as if He had been slain. The Lamb of God still has the marks of His death. (See John 1:29.) He will have them all through eternity. His people will always be reminded of the cost of salvation. But He is standing. For He arose from the dead and is alive forevermore.

This Lamb is different from other lambs. He has seven horns and seven eyes. All through Scripture, horns speak of strength and power. (See 1 Kings 22:11; Zechariah 1:18-19.) This Lamb is not helpless as most lambs are. He is strong and has power to rule all the earth.

The seven eyes tell us that the Lamb is all-wise. (In the Bible, the number seven pictures perfection and completion.) He has all the wisdom of God. (See Colossians 2:3.) And no one is wiser than God!

## Show Illustration #10

This wise and powerful Lamb, God the Son, is the only One worthy to open the scroll. He steps forward and receives the scroll from the hand of God His Father. John stopped crying. He watched with the elders and the living creatures and the angels. This was the moment for which they had all waited. Now they couldn't remain silent.

## 3. THE NEW SONG
### Revelation 5:8-10

## Show Illustration #11

The four living creatures fell down before the Lamb. The 24 elders drop before Him. Each elder held a harp, ready to praise the Lamb with song. (See Psalm 33:2; 98:5.) Each one also held a golden bowl full of incense (perfumed spices for burning in worship). These bowls of incense represented the prayers and praise of all the saints, the people of God. For hundreds of years thousands have prayed: "Thy Kingdom come. Thy will be done in earth, as it is in Heaven" (Matthew 6:10). These prayers were about to be answered.

As the creatures and elders bowed low, they sang a new song–a song that had never been sung before. In it they told the worth of the Lamb. "You are worthy to take the scroll and break its seals. For You were slain. With Your blood You have purchased for God people from every language and tongue and nation. And You have made us to be a kingdom and priests to our God. And [some future day] we'll reign on the earth."

What a mighty song of rejoicing! The Lamb of God had been slain and is alive again. He is the only One who is worthy to open the scroll so the rest of the program of God can be fulfilled. He will rule forever. He will appoint His own who come from every tribe and nation to rule on the earth.

## 4. THE WORSHIPFUL CREATION
### Revelation 5:11-14

John had never heard such a mighty sound of singing. He listened in wonder as the living creatures and the elders and millions of angels exclaim: "Worthy is the Lamb–the Lamb who was slain–to receive all power and riches and wisdom and strength and honor and glory and blessing."

Did you observe that the multitude in Heaven gave seven praises to the Lord Jesus Christ? They said He is worthy to receive (1) power, (2) riches, (3) wisdom, (4) strength, (5) honor, (6) glory and (7) blessing.

## Show Illustration #12

This is not the end of the worship in Heaven. John hears more. He is privileged to look forward to the future. Then every created thing in Heaven, on earth, under the earth and every creature in the sea will worship the Lord Jesus Christ. They will say, "To Him who sits on the throne, and to the Lamb, be blessing and honor and glory and power forever and ever." (Compare with Philippians 2:9-11.) And the four living creatures keep saying, "Amen" [so be it]. Again the 24 elders fall down and worship. What a sight! What a sound!

All of this and more, John saw up in Heaven hundreds of years ago. These things and many others (which are recorded in the book of Revelation) will take place. For they are all in the program of God. And all He has planned will be fulfilled. We'll see some of the marvelous things God has planned for those who belong to His family. We will see, too, the dreadful future of those who refuse to turn to His Son here on earth.

In the beginning of time, God made everything beautiful and perfect. Everything was full of joy and peace and happy singing. The Bible says that "the morning stars sang together, and all the sons of God shouted for joy" (Job 38:7). But sin came. Adam and Eve, the first two people on earth, chose their own way instead of God's way. And choosing one's own way instead of God's, is sin. Sin spoiled everything. And all who have been born since Adam and Eve have chosen his/her own way, rather than God's. So all are slaves of sin and Satan.

Now the whole creation suffers and waits for the day when we shall be freed from the curse of sin. (See Romans 8:21-23) That day is coming. It is in the program of God. God has promised that some future day every person everywhere will bow and acknowledge that Jesus Christ is the Lord of Heaven. (See Philippians 2:10-11.)

For those who have not placed their trust in the Lord Jesus Christ, that will be a dreadful day. They will have to bow before Him. Then they will be cast out from the presence of God to suffer eternal punishment forever and ever.

If you are not a child of God, will you this moment turn to Christ, the Lamb of God? He died and rose again for your sin. Do you believe He is God the Son? (See 1 John 4:15.) Will you ask His forgiveness for your sin? Will you thank Him for dying for you? If so–and if you truly mean it–God will accept you as His child forever.

For you who have already been born into the family of God, there is a glorious future. You will live and rule with Christ on the earth for a thousand years–and then forever But check your life right now. Are you living to please Him so you won't have regrets when you bow before Him and reign with Him? If there is anything you should confess, do it now. Are you sinning by not giving Christ first place in your life? Are you a grumbler, a complainer? Do you not trust God entirely? List in your notebook anything which is not pleasing to God. Decide now what you will do to overcome these sinful habits. Then we'll pray that here on earth our lives–as well as our lips–will be a continual praise to God.

## Lesson 4
# GOD, THE TRINITY, VICTORIOUS

### NOTE TO THE TEACHER

For your own study of the subject of the Trinity, refer to the following Scripture verses.

In Matthew 3:16-17, the Lord Jesus comes up out of the water. The Holy Spirit comes down from Heaven. And God the Father announces that Christ is His much-loved Son.

In Matthew 28:19, Jesus teaches that new Christians are to be baptized in the name of the Father, the Son and the Holy Spirit.

Paul uses the names of the Three-in-One at the close of his second letter to the Corinthians. (See 2 Corinthians 13:14.)

The Father, the Son and the Spirit are each spoken of as God. (See Romans 1:7; Hebrews 1:8; Acts 5:3-4.) Not One of the Three is greater or less than the Others. There cannot be a division among Them.

The Father God of the Three-in-One is not seen. (See John 1:18.)

God the Son of the Three-in-One left Heaven to live in a human body. (See John 1:14-18.)

God the Holy Spirit of the Three-in-One works in and through men. (See 1 Corinthians 2:9-10.)

God is one God in three Persons.

*Teacher:* Review, review, review. Nothing is more important in teaching than to review. To introduce the review of the last lesson, we suggest using the object lesson on page 8 by Charles Ryrie.* It will help your students to understand the meaning of worship. Use a valuable piece of money.

\* From *Easy-to-Give Object Lessons* by Charles C. Ryrie. Used by permission of the publisher, Moody Press, Chicago, IL 60610 USA

**Scripture to be studied:** All Scriptures mentioned in the text.

**The *aim* of the lesson:** To show that God, the Three-in-One, will be victorious.

**What your students should *know*:** A war is going on between God and Satan.

**What your students should *feel*:** Confidence and trust in God, knowing that He is all-powerful.

**What your students should *do*:** Obey God and do His will by spreading the good news of salvation wherever they go.

**Lesson outline (for the teacher's and students' notebooks):**

1. A false god (Judges 16:23-30; 1 Samuel 5:1-12; 6:13).
2. The true God (John 1:14-18; 14:9; 1 Corinthians 2:9-10).
3. The war (Revelation 12:7, 13, 17).
4. The winner (Revelation 11:15; 19:6).

**The verse to be memorized:**

*Thou art worthy, O Lord, to receive glory and honor and power, for Thou hast created all things, and for Thy pleasure they are and were created.* (Revelation 4:11)

## THE LESSON

Do you understand the meaning of the word *worship*? It is "acknowledging the worth of something or someone." Worship is recognizing worth.

Here I have (show and tell what piece of money you have). What is it worth? It's worth a nice coat or (name several things your students would like to have). When you were very young, you didn't know the difference between a penny and a dollar. (Use the names of currency used in your land.) Your parents bought all the things you needed. And money wasn't important to you. Now that you're older you realize how much money it takes to buy the things you want. So money means something to you. You recognize the worth of money by what it can do for you. God wants us to worship Him. (See John 4:24.) That means He wants us to recognize His worth. And what will help us to worship better? Know more about His worth by knowing what He can do.

When children are growing up, they don't need to see money framed and hanging on the wall. As they learn what money can do, they respect its worth. Worship isn't really helped by putting a picture of Christ on the wall to look at. Worship is helped as we learn through experience what Christ can do. When He answers your prayers, when He helps you through temptation, then you realize how great He is. When you recognize His greatness and worth, you will worship Him. In the words of the verse we have been memorizing, you can say from your heart,"You are worthy, O Lord our God, to receive glory and honor and power."

When you're in Heaven, you will worship God. What a great pity it would be to wait until then to do so!

## 1. A FALSE GOD
### Judges 16:23-30; 1 Samuel 5:1-12; 6:13

Many years before John saw the future in Heaven, the Philistine people worshiped a man-made idol called Dagon. They called it "god." Their god had the head and hands of a man and the body of a fish. The Philistines built a special temple for Dagon and offered him sacrifices. They believed that Dagon helped them win battles against their enemies. They praised this idol which they had made with their own hands. (See Judges 16:23-30.)

The Philistines hated the people of Israel. In one war, the Philistines killed 30,000 Israelites! Then they stole the precious ark of God from the people of Israel. This was a tremendous loss, for God spoke to His people from above the ark. (See Exodus 25:22.) The ark was small enough to be carried from place to place. So the Israelites had taken it to war with them. But they lost the battle–and the ark!

The Philistines carried the ark to the temple of Dagon. They set it down beside the idol and left it there for the night. The next morning, when the Philistines came to the temple, they saw their idol lying on its face in front of the ark. They set it up again.

### Show Illustration #13

But the next morning the same thing had happened. Dagon had fallen on its face before the ark. This time its head and hands were broken off.

Soon after this, a terrible sickness came upon the people of Ashdod. Many died. Those who were still alive were afraid. The men said, "The ark of the God of Israel cannot stay with us. His hand is against us and against Dagon, our god."

At last the ark was sent back to the Israelites. When the men of Israel saw the ark coming, they shouted with joy. (See 1 Samuel 5:1-12; 6:13.) God had proved Himself powerful against the enemy.

Years later King Solomon, the wisest man who ever lived (except Jesus Christ, Son of God) said, "Lord God of Israel, there is no God like Thee, in Heaven above or on earth beneath" (1 Kings 8:23). Who is God? Dagon is not God. The ark is not God. But who is the true God?

## 2. THE TRUE GOD
### John 1:14-18; 14:9; 1 Corinthians 2:9-10

Many years ago when men drew only pictures and signs for words, some pictured God as a great eye on a sceptre. (A sceptre is a staff which is carried by a king or ruler.) To them, this meant that God is like an eye and can see everything and everyone all the time.

How would you describe God? What word or words would you use? (*Teacher:* encourage discussion. Have students read John 14:9. Remind them that God the Son took a human body and lived in this world. Through His perfect life, His love, and His goodness, people saw what God is like.)

Dagon was not like the living God. Like other idols, it was made by human hands. But the true God was not made. He had no beginning. He always was and He always will be. He is eternal.

Dagon, the make-believe god, had two parts–part man and part fish. But the everlasting God of Heaven is a Trinity. That means *the unity of three persons in one God*. God is One in three persons: God the Father, God the Son, and God the Holy Spirit. Is this hard to understand? Perhaps. But even if you can't understand it, you can believe it. If we could understand all about God, it would mean that He is no greater than we are. Who would want to worship such a God? It may help you to understand about the Trinity by thinking of the sun.

The great ball above which we call the sun is some 93 million miles away. That is so far that no one has ever been able to see the sun. All we see is the light which comes from it. In the same way, no man has seen God the Father at any time. But we can learn a great deal about the sun by studying the sunlight. So we can learn a great deal about God the Father by getting to know God the Son, the Lord Jesus Christ. Like the sunshine, Jesus is called the brightness (outshining) of God's glory. (See Hebrews 1:3.)

Just as the sunlight is the sun, so Jesus Christ is God. On a cloudy day the sun suddenly shines and we say, "There is the sun!"

We don't mean that the great ball in the sky has come down. That would be foolish. It is the sunlight we see. But the sunlight and the sun are one. We call them both "the sun." So God the Father and God the Son are One. We call both "God" for both are God.

But there is something else in the sun–its chemical power. A few weeks after planting seeds, some shoots appear. What made them grow? The sun–the chemical power in the sunshine–did. That power is distinct from the sun and from the sunlight, yet it is one with them. And we speak of it, too, as "the sun," for it is the sun.

The Holy Spirit is like that. He does not have a body as we do. Yet He is a real person. He speaks; He acts; He prays; He lives in the hearts of many. And He can be grieved. He is a distinct person, yet He is one with God the Father and God the Son. He is God the Holy Spirit. He quietly works in hearts and lives, giving the life of God to those who receive God the Son. (These truths of God, the Three-in-One, are from the introductory material in the *Pilgrim* edition of the Bible. We trust you own a copy of it by now, teacher.)

### Show Illustration #14

When John was taken up to Heaven to see what will happen in the future, he saw God the Father on His throne. The Lamb, God the Son, was at the throne also. And God the Holy Spirit (represented by seven burning lamps) was before the throne.

Looking at the throne, John saw lightning and heard thunder. (See Revelation 4:5.) What did they mean? These were warnings. God is telling us that judgment is coming. In the beginning, God created man to live on earth and be in charge of all that He had created. Man was responsible to rule the earth for God. Everything was good.

## 3. THE WAR
### Revelation 12:7, 13, 17

Then God's great enemy, Satan, came to man and caused him to sin against God. And sin spoiled everything. What a sad day that was!

Originally, Satan was one of God's highest angels. His name was Lucifer. He became so proud of himself that he began to think he was better than God. He even hoped to make himself the king of the universe! He would establish a kingdom of his own. His kingdom would fight against and destroy the kingdom of God.

### Show Illustration #15

He was cast out of Heaven and became the enemy of God and the enemy of all who would ever belong to God's kingdom. His name was changed to *Satan*, which means "adversary" [enemy].

To be a ruler, Satan had to have subjects under him. So he persuaded many angels to join him. He became prince of demons and prince of the power of the air. (See Matthew 12:24-26; Ephesians 2:2; 1 John 5:19.) But he wanted an earthly kingdom. So he came to man to turn him against God. That is what happened in the Garden of Eden. Adam and Eve rejected God's rule and were brought under the rulership of a new king, Satan. The first King, God, is loving and kind. He offered Adam and Eve life and peace and happiness in return for willing obedience. But how different Satan is! He is hard and selfish. He gave Adam and Eve sickness, sorrow and death in return for service to him.

So ever since then, there have been two kingdoms–God's kingdom and Satan's kingdom. And the two are always at war. The kingdom of Satan continually attacks the kingdom of God, trying to destroy it. This war is being fought in Heaven and on earth. (See Ephesians 6:10-12; Revelation 12:7, 13, 17.)

God, with all His mighty power, could have defeated Satan at the very beginning. But because He is all-wise and loving, He gives men and women, boys and girls, the opportunity to make a choice. Each may choose the kingdom to which he/she wants to belong.

The battle continues today. Satan wants to rule earth and Heaven. God wants to rule earth and Heaven. Who will win? Can you guess?

## 4. THE WINNER
**Revelation 11:15; 19:6**

Do you remember the scroll which John saw in Heaven? In it is the program of God for the future. The scroll was in the hand of God the Father. The Lord Jesus Christ, the strong Lion of Judah (Who is also the living Lamb who had been slain), is the only One worthy to take the scroll and open the seals. By His death on the cross, He paid the price to bring people into the kingdom of God. This is how much we mean to him. And this is how much He wants us to be on His side.

But Satan doesn't give up. Dagon, the false god of the Philistines, fell and broke apart in the presence of the true and living God. Dagon and all the idols of earth represent Satan. Satan will try to get you to worship anything and anyone except the true and living God of Heaven. And Satan has power. He's clever. He deceives people. He gets many to listen to him and obey him. Indeed, more people on earth today listen to Satan rather than listen to God.

God will not force you to choose Him as your Master and follow Him. But the Bible tells us that a day is coming when everyone will bow before the Lord Jesus Christ. Then Satan and all who have followed him, will be defeated and cast into the lake of fire to be tormented forever. (See Revelation 20:10-15.) Then the war between God and Satan will be over. And the Lord God–the Three-in-One–will reign forever. (See Revelation 11:15; 19:6.)

### Show Illustration #16

The thunder and flashing lightning from the throne of God in Heaven remind us that God, the Creator of all, will some day be Judge of all He created. (See Genesis 18:25.) He will judge and punish forever all who have refused Him and His Son. (We shall learn about these judgments in our next lessons.)

The only way to escape the judgment of God is to place your trust in the Saviour, God the Son. Will you turn to Him and receive Him into your heart and life? If you will, the Holy Spirit of God will come to live in your life. And God will be your heavenly Father. Only then will you be able to say, "You are worthy, O Lord, to receive glory and honor and power. For You have created all things. And for Your pleasure they are and were created" (Revelation 4:11).

Are you a member of God's family? If so, how many of those living around you know by your life and your lips that you belong to Him? How many of your friends and family know how to become children of God? Don't keep this good news to yourself. If you love the Lord, you'll want to share it with others so they too can be on the winning side forever.

List in your notebook the names of those you want to introduce to the Lord Jesus Christ this week. Decide now how you will make time for this important business.

www.ingramcontent.com/pod-product-compliance
Lightning Source LLC
Chambersburg PA
CBHW060804090426
42736CB00002B/148